The Book of the Secrets of Enoch

A Visionary Journey Through Heaven and Divine Mysteries

A Modern Translation

Adapted for the Contemporary Reader

Enoch the Patriarch

Translated by Tim Zengerink

© **Copyright 2025**
All rights reserved.

It is not legal to reproduce, duplicate, or transmit any part of this document in either electronic means or in printed format. Recording of this publication is strictly prohibited and any storage of this document is not allowed unless with written permission from the publisher except for the use of brief quotations in a book review.

This book contains works of fiction. Any resemblance to persons living or dead, or places, events, or locations is purely coincidental.

Table Of Contents

Preface - Message to the Reader 1
Introduction 5
The Son of Ared; A Man Wise and Beloved of
    God 12

    Chapters I. 2 - II.2 13
    Chapters II.3 - VII. 1 14
    Charters VII. 2 - VIII. 5 16
    Chapters VIII. 6 - X. 2 17
    Chapters X.3 - XI.1 19
    Chapters XI. 2 - XII.I 20
    Chapters XII. 2 - XIII. 5 21
    Chapters XIV. 1 - XV. 4 22
    Chapter XVI.17 23
    Chapters XVI. 8 - XVIII. 3 25
    Chapters XVIII. 4 - XIX. 2 27
    Chapters XIX. 3 - XX. 3 28
    Chapters XX. 4—XXII. 5 30
    Chapters XXII. 6 - XXIII. 4 32
    Chapters XXIII. 5 - XXIV. 5 33
    Chapters XXV. 1 - XXVII. 1 35
    Chapters XXVII. 2 - XXIX. 3 36
    Chapters XXIX. 4 - XXX. 3 38

- Chapter XXX. 48 39
- Chapter XXX. 915 40
- Chapter XXX. 16, 17 41
- Chapters XXX. 18 - XXXIII.1 43
- Chapter XXXIII. 26 43
- Chapters XXXIII. 7 - XXXV. 1 45
- Chapters XXXV.2 - XXXIX. 1 46
- Chapters XXXIX. 2 - XL. 6 49
- CHAPTER XL. 713 51
- Chapters XLI. 1 - XLII. 6 52
- Chapters XLII. 7 - XLIII. 2 54
- Chapters XLIII. 3 - XLF. 4 55
- Chapters XLVI. 1 - XLVIII. 1 56
- Chapters XLVIII. 2 - XLIX.1 58
- Chapters XLIX. 2 - LI. 2 59
- Chapters LI. 3 - LIII. 1 61
- Chapters LIII. 2 - LVI. 1 62
- Chapters LVI. 2 - LVIII. 5 63
- Chapters LVIII. 6 - LIX. 4 65
- Chapters LIX. 5 - LXII. 1 67
- Chapters LXII. 2 - LXV.2 69
- Chapters LXV.2 - LXVI.1 71

Thank You for Reading 74

Preface - Message to the Reader

What If You Could Help Rebuild the Greatest Library in Human History?

Thousands of years ago, the Library of Alexandria stood as the crown jewel of human achievement — a sanctuary where the collected wisdom of every known civilization was gathered, preserved, and shared freely.

And then, it was lost.

Through fire, conquest, and the slow erosion of time, humanity lost not just books — but ideas, dreams, discoveries, and stories that could have changed the world forever.

Today, the Library of Alexandria lives again — and you are invited to be a part of its restoration.

Our mission is simple yet profound:

To rebuild the greatest library the world has ever known, and to translate all timeless works into every language and dialect, so that no seeker of knowledge is ever left behind again.

By joining our movement to rebuild the modern Library of Alexandria, you become part of an unprecedented mission:

- **Unlimited Access to the Greatest Audiobooks & eBooks Ever Written:**

    Instantly explore thousands of legendary works—Plato, Shakespeare, Jane Austen, Leo Tolstoy, and countless more. All instantly available to read or listen, placing a complete literary universe at your fingertips.

- **Beautiful Paperback & Deluxe Editions at Printing Cost**

    Own any title as an elegant paperback, deluxe hardcover, or stunning collectible boxset—offered to you at true printing cost, delivered straight to your door. Build your personal Library of Alexandria, crafted for beauty, built for durability, and worthy of proud display.

- **Fresh Translations for Modern Readers—in Every Language & Dialect**

    Enjoy timeless masterpieces reimagined in clear, contemporary language—no more outdated phrases or obscure references. Alongside the original versions, we're tirelessly translating these classics into every language and dialect imaginable, ensuring accessibility and understanding across cultures and generations.

- **Join a Global Renaissance of Literature & Knowledge**

    You directly support expanding our library, publishing deluxe editions at true cost, translating works into all global languages, and bringing humanity's greatest stories to people everywhere. By joining today, you're not just preserving a legacy of masterpieces; you set in motion a powerful wave of literary accessibility.

Become a Torchbearer of Knowledge.

Join us for free now at **LibraryofAlexandria.com**

Together, we will ensure that the light of human wisdom never fades again.

With gratitude and a shared love of knowledge,

The Modern Library of Alexandria Team

Visit:

www.libraryofalexandria.com

Or scan the code below:

Introduction

Enoch's Ascent and the Mystery of the Heavens

Among the great visionary texts of antiquity, few are as rich in spiritual wonder or mystical depth as The Book of the Secrets of Enoch, also known as 2 Enoch or Slavonic Enoch. Attributed to the enigmatic figure of Enoch, the seventh generation from Adam, this apocalyptic and mystical work transports the reader into a cosmos teeming with divine presence, angelic hierarchies, and eternal truths. It invites us to ascend beyond the material world and explore the layered architecture of the heavens as revealed to one of the most righteous men in biblical tradition. This is not just a text of theological interest—it is a spiritual voyage, a revelation wrapped in poetic mystery, and a profound meditation on creation, morality, and divine justice.

Unlike 1 Enoch, which is more widely known and preserved in the Ethiopic tradition, 2 Enoch survived primarily in Old Church Slavonic and was rediscovered in the 19th century. Its obscurity for centuries only adds to its sense of hiddenness and wonder. Though not part of most biblical canons, it was clearly held in high regard by the communities that preserved it. The text likely originated in the first century CE, possibly in a Jewish context influenced by Hellenistic thought, and it reflects a time of profound spiritual searching and cosmic speculation. It offers an account of Enoch's journey through the ten heavens, his direct encounters with angelic beings, and the revelations imparted to him by God Himself—revelations concerning not only the structure of the cosmos but also the purpose of life, the nature of sin, and the final destiny of souls.

The ascent begins when Enoch, already known as a righteous man who "walked with God" in the Book of Genesis, is taken by two angels at God's command. What follows is an unparalleled journey through realms unseen, each higher heaven more radiant, more awe-inspiring, and more spiritually intense than the last. In each level, Enoch learns something new about the divine order of creation: the movements of celestial bodies, the organization of angelic hosts, the secrets of time and seasons, the storehouses of snow and light, and the moral laws that govern both heaven and earth. The journey culminates in the tenth heaven, where Enoch is granted a direct vision of the face of God—a moment so transcendent that even the angelic hosts cover their faces in awe.

Yet the text is not content to remain in the abstract. Interwoven with these cosmic revelations are deeply ethical teachings. Enoch is shown the consequences of righteousness and wickedness, the coming judgment of God, and the moral responsibilities placed upon humanity. He is charged to bring these teachings back to earth and pass them on to his children before he is taken from the world. What emerges is a work that unites mystical vision with moral urgency. The grandeur of the cosmos is not just to be admired, but to be understood as a mirror of divine order—one that demands a corresponding order in the lives of human beings.

The Structure of Divine Reality

One of the most compelling features of The Book of the Secrets of Enoch is its vision of the cosmos as a sacred, ordered structure. The ten heavens are not arbitrary layers but expressions of divine intentionality. Each level has a specific function and reflects a different facet of God's creative power and moral governance. This multilayered vision of the universe echoes ancient cosmologies found in Mesopotamian, Persian, and Hellenistic traditions, but it is uniquely filtered through a Jewish theological lens that affirms the unity and sovereignty of the Creator.

In the first heaven, Enoch sees the angels who watch over the stars and the storehouses of snow and dew. In the second, he witnesses a dark place where fallen angels are imprisoned in torment—a warning of divine judgment. As he ascends, each heaven reveals more of the divine economy: angels who govern seasons and the natural world, others who record human deeds, and still others who serve before the face of God in perpetual praise. The seventh and eighth heavens are particularly sacred, reserved for those who were righteous on earth and for angelic powers of the highest order. The ninth heaven houses the innermost purposes of God—hidden even from the angels. Finally, in the tenth heaven, Enoch beholds the throne of God and receives mysteries no human being had ever been granted.

These descriptions are not merely ornamental. They reflect a profound conviction that the universe is not a meaningless expanse but a spiritual hierarchy infused with divine presence. Everything has its place, everything serves a purpose, and everything is subject to moral law. The text insists that what is true above is true below: just as the heavens operate in harmonious obedience to God, so too should humanity. Disorder in human life is not only rebellion but disharmony with the very structure of the cosmos.

This cosmological vision is inseparable from the book's moral instruction. Enoch is repeatedly reminded that knowledge of divine mysteries comes with responsibility. He is not taken into the heavens merely for his own enlightenment, but so that he might teach others. Throughout the text, he exhorts his children and descendants to pursue righteousness, avoid sin, and live in accordance with God's commands. The grandeur of his vision is meant to awaken moral clarity, not spiritual pride. The more one sees of God's world, the more one is called to humility and obedience.

In this way, The Book of the Secrets of Enoch embodies a fusion of mystical insight and prophetic authority. It does not draw a line between the visionary and the ethical, but integrates them. To see the divine is to be changed by it, and to be changed is to act accordingly. The ultimate goal of revelation is transformation—of the individual, of the community, and of the world.

Reading the Text as a Spiritual Journey

To read The Book of the Secrets of Enoch well is to read it not merely as an ancient document, but as a guide to inner ascent. Its heavenly journey can be read as a map of the soul's potential: a call to rise above the distractions of the world and align oneself with divine truth. The multiple heavens, the angelic beings, the vast storehouses of elements and light—all these can be seen not only as cosmological descriptions but as metaphors for levels of consciousness, degrees of spiritual maturity, and the layers of reality that we are invited to explore through prayer, reflection, and righteous living.

This modern translation has been created to make this profound and visionary work accessible to contemporary readers without sacrificing its poetic depth or symbolic richness. The archaic language and difficult syntax of older versions have been carefully revised into clear, vivid, and faithful English, sentence by sentence, to preserve the original intent while enhancing readability. Great care has been taken to retain the sacred tone and mystical atmosphere that make this text so powerful.

As you read, take your time. Let each heaven unfold like a step in your own journey. Reflect on the moral teachings as if they were addressed to you directly. Consider the awe and humility that Enoch felt as he encountered each new revelation. And most importantly, do not treat this book as merely an intellectual curiosity or an ancient artifact. Read it as a living document—a spiritual invitation to align your life with the divine structure of creation.

The Book of the Secrets of Enoch offers no easy answers, no simple formulas. Instead, it offers a path—one walked by a man who dared to approach the face of God and returned with a message of awe, order, and judgment. It reminds us that the universe is not blind, that righteousness matters, and that the soul is called not just to believe, but to ascend. Let this book inspire you, challenge you, and guide you upward, through the heavens, toward the mysteries of the divine.

The Son of Ared;
A Man Wise and Beloved of God

[Concerning the Life and the Dream of Enoch]

There was once a very wise man who achieved great things. God loved him deeply and chose him to see the heavenly realms, the places of wisdom, and the eternal, unchanging God. He was shown the Lord of all—glorious, bright, and beyond imagination. He saw the shining presence of God's servants, the throne that no one can approach, and the countless spiritual beings who serve the Lord. He witnessed their different forms, heard their indescribable songs, and saw the vastness of the universe.

At that time, he said, "When I was 165 years old, my son Methuselah was born. After that, I lived another 200 years, making my total lifespan 365 years."

On the first day of the first month, I was alone in my house. I lay down on my bed and fell asleep. As I slept, a deep sadness filled my heart, and I began to weep in my dream. I didn't understand why I was feeling this way or what was about to happen to me.

Then, two men appeared before me. They were very

tall, unlike any humans I had ever seen. Their faces shone like the sun, their eyes burned like torches, and fire came from their mouths. Their clothes looked like they were made of feathers, their feet glowed purple, and their wings were brighter than gold. Their hands were as white as snow. They stood by my bed and called me by my name.

I woke up and saw them clearly standing in front of me. I was terrified and quickly bowed before them. My face changed because of the fear I felt.

The men said to me, "Do not be afraid, Enoch. Be strong. The eternal God has sent us to you. Today, you will go with us into heaven."

They continued, "Tell your sons, your servants, and everyone in your household not to search for you until the Lord returns you to them."

I quickly did as they said and left my house. I called my sons—Methuselah, Regim, and Gaidal—and told them everything these two men had said to me.

Chapters I. 2 - II.2

Listen to me, my children, because I do not know where I am going or what will happen to me. I ask you now, my children, do not turn away from God. Stay faithful to the Lord and follow His ways. Do not worship useless idols that did not create the heavens and the earth, because they will be destroyed along with those who follow them.

May God give you strength to remain faithful and always respect Him. And now, my children, do not search for me until the Lord returns me to you.

After I finished speaking to my sons, the two men who had appeared to me called me to them. They lifted me up on their wings and placed me on the clouds. The clouds began to rise, carrying me higher and higher.

As I ascended, I looked down and saw the air far below me. As we went even higher, I entered a new place beyond the sky. The men brought me to the first heaven, where they showed me a vast and powerful sea—much larger than any sea on earth.

Chapters II.3 - VII. 1

They brought me before the elders and leaders in charge of the stars, showing me two hundred angels who guide the stars and make sure they follow their paths in the sky. These angels had wings and moved in circles around the stars, keeping them in their correct places.

Then I looked and saw huge storehouses filled with snow and ice, guarded by angels who watched over these powerful treasures. I also saw where the clouds were kept, the place where they form and where they return.

Next, they showed me the storehouses of the dew, which looked like a fine, anointing oil. Its colors were as beautiful and varied as all the colors on earth. Many angels were assigned to guard these places, opening and closing them at the right times.

The men who were guiding me then took me to the second heaven. There, I saw a dark and dreadful place where prisoners were hanging, waiting for eternal judgment. These angels were filled with sorrow and despair, darker than the deepest shadow on earth. They cried out constantly, their voices filled with pain.

I asked the men with me, "Why are these beings suffering endlessly?" They answered, "These are the ones who turned away from the Lord. They refused to follow His commands and chose their own ways instead. They rebelled with their leader, and now they are imprisoned here in the second heaven."

I felt deep pity for them. Then, to my surprise, the angels turned toward me, bowed, and said, "Man of God, pray to the Lord for us." But I answered, "Who am I, a mere human, to pray for angels? I don't even know where I am going or what will happen to me. I don't even know who could pray for me."

Charters VII. 2 - VIII. 5

[Of the taking of Enoch to the third Heaven 2.]

The men then took me to the third heaven. They placed me in the middle of a breathtaking garden, a place more beautiful than anything I had ever seen.

I saw trees of every color, full of ripe, sweet-smelling fruit that filled the air with a wonderful fragrance. There was an endless supply of food, each kind giving off its own pleasant scent.

At the center of the garden stood the Tree of Life, where God Himself rests when He visits Paradise. This tree was beyond words, its beauty unmatched. It gave off a heavenly fragrance, and its appearance shone like gold, deep red, and something like glowing fire, radiating light all around.

From its roots, four streams flowed—one of honey, one of milk, one of oil, and one of wine. These streams moved gently, spreading out in four directions. They flowed toward the Paradise of Eden, existing between the worlds of the living and the eternal, and continued their course across the earth, moving in harmony with the rest of creation.

There was also an olive tree that never stopped producing oil. Every tree in this garden bore fruit, and each one was overflowing with blessings.

Three hundred glorious angels guarded the garden, singing songs of praise without end. Their voices filled the air, offering worship to the Lord every day. I was amazed by the beauty of this place and said, "What an incredibly blessed place this is!" The men who were with me answered.

Chapters VIII. 6 - X. 2

[The showing to Enoch of the Righteous, and the Place of Prayer]

"This place, Enoch, has been prepared for the righteous. It is for those who have endured many hardships and attacks in their lives, yet have remained strong. It is for those who turn away from evil and choose to do what is right. It belongs to those who feed the hungry, clothe those in need, help the weak, and care for orphans who have no one to protect them. It is for those who live blamelessly before the Lord and serve Him with all their hearts. This is their eternal reward, a place of peace prepared just for them."

Then the men took me to the northern side, where I saw a place so terrifying that words could not describe it. It was filled with unbearable suffering. Thick darkness covered everything, and it was impossible to see through the heavy gloom. There was no light, only a fierce and never-ending fire. A river of flames flowed through it without stopping. The entire place was surrounded by burning fire, yet at the same time, there were icy winds and freezing cold. It was a place of both unbearable heat and bitter cold.

Inside this terrible place were prisoners who looked wild and tormented. The angels guarding them were fierce and showed no mercy. They carried terrifying weapons and punished the prisoners without relief. I cried out, "Oh no! This place is horrifying!"

The men with me answered, "This place, Enoch, is for those who have rejected God and lived wickedly on earth.

"It is for those who have committed terrible sins, practiced witchcraft, and used dark magic. It is for those who took pride in their evil actions, stole from others, spread lies, and caused harm out of jealousy. It is for those who lived in impurity, committed murder, and took advantage of the weak.

"This place belongs to those who let the hungry starve when they could have fed them and left the poor without clothing when they had the power to help. It is for those who did not acknowledge their Creator but instead worshiped idols—lifeless objects that cannot see or hear. These false gods were made by human hands, yet they bowed down to them as if they had power.

"For all these people, this place has been prepared as their eternal punishment."

Chapters X.3 - XI.1

[Here they took Enoch to the fourth Heaven, where is the Course of the Sun and Moon.]

The men then took me to the fourth heaven, where they showed me how the sun and moon move along their paths. I saw how bright their light was and measured their courses. I learned that the sun's light is seven times stronger than the moon's. I watched as they traveled in their orbits, moving quickly like a rushing wind. They never stopped, continuing their journey day and night without rest.

I saw four large stars moving alongside the sun. Each of these stars had a thousand smaller stars following on its right side, and another four stars had a thousand stars each on their left side. In total, there were eight thousand stars surrounding the sun.

Around the sun, I saw an enormous group of angels—fifteen myriads of them—who traveled with it during the day, guiding and watching over it. At night, a thousand angels took their place to accompany it.

Each of these angels had six wings, and they flew in front of the sun's chariot, leading and directing its path.

A hundred other angels were given the task of keeping the sun warm and bright, making sure its light and heat reached the earth. It was an incredible sight, a breathtaking display of heavenly order and divine power.

Chapters XI. 2 - XII.I

[Of the wonderful Creatures of the Sun.]

I looked and saw amazing flying creatures, unlike anything I had ever seen before. They were called phoenixes and chalkadri, and their appearance was both incredible and strange. These creatures had the feet and tails of lions, but their heads looked like crocodiles. Their bodies shimmered with a purple glow, shining like a bright rainbow. Each one was enormous, measuring nine hundred units in size.

They had wings like angels, with twelve large and powerful wings each. These creatures served the sun's chariot, traveling alongside it on its journey. They carried out tasks given to them by God, bringing heat and dew to the earth as commanded.

As the sun moved along its path, these creatures followed, guiding its way beneath the sky and through the hidden places under the earth. The sun's light never stopped shining, constantly moving to brighten the world and sustain life below.

Chapters XII. 2 - XIII. 5

[The Angels took Enoch, and placed him on the East at the Gates of the Sun.]

The men took me to the East, where they showed me the gates through which the sun rises at different times. The sun follows a set pattern based on the changing seasons, the months of the year, and the hours of day and night.

I saw six enormous gates, each carefully measured. They were massive, with each gate measuring sixty-one stadia and a quarter of a stadium. I measured them myself and confirmed their enormous size. These gates are where the sun begins its journey, moving westward and following a path that changes with the months and seasons.

The sun travels through the first gate for forty-two days, then through the second gate for thirty-five days. It moves through the fourth and fifth gates for thirty-five days each. However, when it passes through the sixth gate, it stays there for forty-five days.

After that, the sun reverses its path, returning from the sixth gate. It moves through the fifth gate for thirty-five days, then the fourth gate for thirty-five days, followed by the third gate for thirty-five days, and finally through the second gate for another thirty-five days.

This completes the full year, with all the days perfectly matching the sun's cycle and the changes in the four seasons.

Chapters XIV. 1 - XV. 4

[They took Enock to the West.]

The men then took me to the western part of the sky and showed me six huge open gates. These gates were just like the ones in the East, and through them, the sun sets after completing its journey across the 365 days and a quarter of a day in a year.

As the sun passes through the Western gates, 400 angels come to take its crown and bring it before the Lord. The sun, traveling in its chariot, remains without its light for seven full hours during the night. But when it reaches the East during the eighth hour, the 400 angels return its crown and place it back on the sun.

At that moment, the Phoenixes and Chalkidri, special creatures of the sun, begin to sing. Because of their song, all the birds in the world flap their wings with joy, praising the giver of light. These creatures sing at the Lord's command.

The sun then rises again, spreading its light across the entire earth. The men explained to me how the sun's movements are measured and showed me the gates through which it enters and exits. These great gates were designed by God to mark the passing of days and to set the cycle of the year.

This is why the sun is so large and plays such an important role in the order of the world.

Chapter XVI.17

[The Men· took Enoch and placed him at the East, at the Course of the Moon.]

The men then explained to me how the moon's movements are calculated. They showed me its paths and cycles, pointing out twelve large gates stretching from west to east. The moon enters and exits through these gates at its set times.

The moon moves through the first gate when the sun is in the west, staying there for exactly thirty-one days. It also spends thirty-one days in the second gate. In the third and fourth gates, it remains for thirty days each. It continues this pattern, staying in the fifth and sixth gates for thirty-one days, in the seventh gate for thirty days, in the eighth and ninth gates for thirty-one days, in the tenth gate for thirty days, in the eleventh for thirty-one days, and in the twelfth for twenty-eight days. This cycle repeats as the moon moves through the western gates, following the same pattern as the eastern gates, completing the year.

Translated by Tim Zengerink

The sun's yearly cycle is 365 days and a quarter, but the lunar year is only 354 days, made up of twelve months of twenty-nine days each. This leaves an extra eleven days that must be added to match the sun's full cycle for the year. These additional days, called lunar epacts, make up the difference between the sun and the moon's cycles.

Over three years, the extra quarter day from each year is ignored, but in the fourth year, the missing time is accounted for. That is why three years seem to be missing days, but in the fourth year, everything aligns again. To keep the calculations correct, two extra months are added over time, while others are slightly adjusted to maintain balance.

Once the moon completes its cycle through the western gates, it returns to the eastern gates, bringing its light. It moves constantly, both day and night, traveling along its set path faster than the winds of the sky. Alongside it are spirits, creatures, and angels, each with six wings, who guide its movements.

Seven months of the moon's cycle are also measured within a larger cycle of nineteen years, ensuring that everything in the sky stays in perfect order.

Chapters XVI. 8 - XVIII. 3

In the middle of the heavens, I saw a vast army of angels, armed and ready to serve the Lord. They played cymbals and organs, and their voices rose in endless songs of praise. The sound was unlike anything I had ever heard—so beautiful and powerful that it stirred my soul with joy.

Then, the men guiding me led me further and took me up to the fifth heaven. There, I saw an enormous crowd, too many to count. These were the Grigori, and while they looked like men, they were much larger, even bigger than giants.

Their faces looked tired and sorrowful, and they were completely silent. The entire place felt heavy and lifeless—there was no worship, no joy, and no service to the Lord. Confused, I turned to the men who brought me there and asked, "Why do these beings look so sad and lifeless? Why are they silent, and why is there no worship here?"

They answered, "These are the Grigori. Long ago, they and their leader, Satanail, turned away from the Lord. Because of their rebellion, they were cast into great darkness in the second heaven. Three of them were sent down from God's throne to a place called Ermon. There, at Mount Iermon, they saw the daughters of men, found them beautiful, and took them as wives.

By doing this, they disobeyed God and brought corruption to the earth. They abandoned their duties and went against His will. Their children became giants, men of great size and strength, but their existence only brought wickedness and chaos. Sin and lawlessness spread everywhere because of them.

Because of their actions, God passed a severe judgment on them. Now, they mourn for their fallen brothers, knowing they will face punishment on the great and terrible day of the Lord."

Hearing this, I turned to the Grigori and said, "I have seen what happened to your brothers and the suffering they endure. I prayed for them, but the Lord has decided they must remain trapped under the earth until the heavens and the earth pass away. They will never be set free."

I continued, "Why are you waiting, my brothers? Why do you not serve before the Lord? Why do you not fulfill your duties and give Him the honor He deserves instead of continuing in your rebellion?"

When I finished speaking, the Grigori listened to my words. They arranged themselves into four groups within the heaven. As I stood with the men who guided me, four trumpets sounded together, filling the air with a deep and powerful sound. Then, the Grigori began to sing as one. Their voices were filled with sorrow, but their song was soft and moving. Their mournful song rose up before the Lord, carrying their regret and longing for redemption.

Chapters XVIII. 4 - XIX. 2

[The taking up of Enoch, i1tto the sixth, Heaven.]

The men guiding me then took me further and brought me to the sixth heaven. There, I saw seven groups of angels, each one glowing with incredible brightness. Their faces shone even brighter than the sun's rays, and their beauty was beyond anything I had ever seen. They all looked the same, with no differences in their appearance, expressions, or clothing. They stood together in perfect unity.

These angels were responsible for studying and organizing the movements of the stars, the phases of the moon, and the paths of the sun. They ensured that balance was kept in the world, controlling both good and bad conditions as they had been commanded. They also arranged teachings and instructions and created beautiful songs and melodies filled with praise and glory.

These angels were archangels, the leaders over all the other angels. They had authority over everything, both in heaven and on earth. Some were in charge of keeping track of the changing seasons and the passing of years. Others watched over the rivers and seas, making sure the waters flowed as they should. There were also angels who oversaw the growth of plants and trees, ensuring that all living creatures received the food they needed.

I also saw angels who were responsible for recording the lives and actions of every person on earth. They carefully wrote down everything before the Lord, making sure that no deed—good or bad—was ever forgotten.

In the middle of these angels, I saw seven phoenixes, seven cherubim, and seven other beings with six wings each. Together, they sang in perfect harmony with one voice. Their song was so beautiful and powerful that words could not describe it. It was a joyful offering to the Lord, rising up to His holy throne as a tribute to His greatness and glory.

Chapters XIX. 3 - XX. 3

[Thence Enoch is taken into the seventh. Heaven]

The men guiding me took me even higher, bringing me to the seventh heaven. There, I saw a breathtaking and brilliant light. Surrounding it were powerful archangels, spirits of great strength, rulers, and other mighty beings. I saw cherubim and seraphim, shining thrones, and countless watchful eyes. In front of me stood ten groups of radiant beings, each more dazzling than the last. The sight was so overwhelming that I trembled in fear, unable to fully comprehend what I was seeing.

Sensing my fear, the men with me held me and reassured me, saying, "Do not be afraid, Enoch. Be at peace." Their words comforted me, and I was able to stand among them.

Then, they showed me the Lord from a distance, seated on His magnificent and exalted throne. His presence was beyond words—majestic and awe-inspiring. Around Him, all the heavenly beings were gathered, each standing on one of ten steps, perfectly arranged according to their rank. They bowed before the Lord, showing Him deep reverence and honor.

After paying their respects, they returned to their places. With joy and devotion, they stood in the endless light of His presence. In soft and harmonious voices, they sang praises, glorifying the Lord and serving Him with love and honor in the brilliance of His unending glory.

Translated by Tim Zengerink

Chapters XX. 4—XXII. 5

[How the Angels placed Enoch there at the limits of the seventh Heaven and departed from him invisibly.]

They never leave, day or night, but remain before the Lord, carrying out His commands. Surrounding His throne are the cherubim and seraphim, along with six-winged beings who cover His throne with their presence. They sing softly, their voices full of reverence, proclaiming, "Holy, Holy, Holy, Lord God of Hosts! Heaven and earth are filled with Your glory!"

After witnessing these incredible things, the men who had guided me turned to me and said, "Enoch, our task is complete." Then they departed, leaving me alone. Standing at the edge of heaven, fear overtook me. I fell on my face, trembling, and cried out in distress, "What is happening to me?"

But the Lord, in His mercy, sent one of His great archangels—Gabriel. Gabriel spoke gently to me, saying, "Be at peace, Enoch. Do not be afraid. Stand up and follow me, for you will always remain before the Lord." Though his words were meant to calm me, I answered, "O Lord, my spirit is overwhelmed with fear. Please send back the men who brought me here. They were my companions, and with them, I would feel safe to approach You."

Gabriel, however, swiftly lifted me as if I were a leaf carried by the wind. He brought me directly before the Lord. Overcome with awe, I fell on my face and worshiped Him. Then the Lord Himself spoke to me, saying, "Be at peace, Enoch. Do not fear. Stand before Me, for you will remain in My presence forever."

Then Michael, the chief of the archangels, approached and lifted me up. He presented me before the Lord, and the Lord commanded His heavenly servants, "Let Enoch stand before Me forever." The glorious beings bowed low before the Lord and answered, "Let it be done according to Your word, O Lord."

Then the Lord turned to Michael and said, "Remove Enoch's earthly garments and anoint him with My holy oil. Then clothe him in the robe of My glory." Michael obeyed. He took away my earthly robe and anointed me with oil that shone brighter than the sun. The oil smelled sweeter than the finest myrrh, felt cool like morning dew, and glowed with brilliant light. Then he dressed me in garments that radiated with divine glory.

As I looked at myself, I saw that I had been transformed. I was now like the glorious beings who serve the Lord, and all fear and trembling left me.

Then the Lord called upon another archangel, Vretil, who was known for his wisdom and for recording all of the Lord's works. The Lord said to him, "Bring the books from My storehouses and give Enoch a reed to write. Teach him the knowledge contained in these books."

Vretil obeyed immediately, bringing books that smelled of myrrh and handing me a reed. With patience and wisdom, he prepared to teach me the mysteries written within those sacred texts.

Chapters XXII. 6 - XXIII. 4

[Of the writing of Enoch how he wrote about his wonderful Goings and the heavenly Visions, and he himself wrote 366 Book.]

He showed me how the heavens, the earth, and the seas work. He explained the movement of their elements, the rumble of thunder, the paths of the sun and moon, and the way the stars travel and change. He described the cycles of the seasons and years, the passage of days and hours, the way the winds move, the countless angels in heaven, and the beautiful songs they sing in perfect harmony.

He also revealed everything about people—their lives, their different languages, the songs they sing, their knowledge, and the lessons they follow. He shared the melodies of their voices and all the wisdom they need to understand.

For thirty days and thirty nights, Vretil taught me without stopping, speaking the entire time. And for those same thirty days and nights, I wrote without resting, recording everything he told me.

Then, when the time came, Vretil said to me, "You have written everything I have taught you. Now, write about the souls of all people—the souls that have not yet been born and the places that have been prepared for them for eternity. Every soul was created to live forever, even before the world was made."

I obeyed, writing without stopping for another thirty days and nights. By the time I finished, I had written 366 books, carefully recording everything I had seen and learned.

Chapters XXIII. 5 - XXIV. 5

[Of the great Secrets of God, Which God revealed and told to Enoch, and spoke with him Face to Face.]

The Lord called me and said, "Enoch, sit at My left side with Gabriel." I bowed down in deep respect before Him.

Then the Lord spoke again, saying, "Enoch, everything you see—whether still or moving—was created by Me. Now, I will show you how I made everything from nothing and how the visible world came from the unseen.

Even My angels do not know these secrets. I have not told them how creation began, and they do not understand the endless greatness of My works, which I am revealing to you today.

Before anything existed, I alone moved through the unseen, just as the sun moves across the sky from east to west. But unlike the sun, which has a place to rest, I never stopped, for I was constantly creating. I shaped the foundation of everything and began to bring visible things into being."

Then the Lord continued, "I commanded the deep abyss so that things could emerge from the invisible. From this unseen realm, Adoil appeared before Me—vast and magnificent, glowing with a brilliant red light.

I said to Adoil, 'Break open, and let what is inside you be seen.' He obeyed, and a great light burst forth. I was surrounded by this brilliant light, and from within it, the entire world was revealed, just as I had planned. I saw that it was good.

Then I made a throne for Myself and sat upon it. I commanded the light, 'Rise high and become the foundation for everything above.' The light obeyed, ascending to the highest place. As I sat on My throne, I looked at the light and marveled at how great it was."

Chapters XXV. 1 - XXVII. 1

[God again calls from the Depths and there came Arkhas, Tazhis, and one who is very red.]

I called out again into the emptiness and said, "Let something solid and visible come from what cannot be seen." In response, Arkhas appeared—thick, heavy, and glowing with a deep red color.

I told Arkhas, "Separate, and let what comes from you be seen." When he split apart, a vast and shadowy world was revealed—huge, dark, and endless—bringing the beginning of everything below.

I saw that this was good. I commanded, "Go down and become the base for all that will be beneath." And so it happened. Arkhas sank, became firm, and formed the foundation for everything below. Beyond this darkness, there was nothing more.

Translated by Tim Zengerink

Chapters XXVII. 2 - XXIX. 3

[How God established the Water, and surrounded it with Light, and established upon it Seven Islands.]

I commanded the light and darkness to be separated and said, "Let there be something thick and solid." And so it appeared. I spread this new substance out, forming water beneath the light, covering the darkness below.

I made the waters firm, shaping the deep places, and surrounded them with light. Then, I created seven layers, making them clear and strong—both smooth and rough—like glass and ice. I set paths for the waters and other elements, guiding them to move in harmony with the seven stars, each within its own part of the sky. I saw that this was good.

I separated light from darkness and divided the waters above from those below. I told the light, "You will be called day," and the darkness, "You will be called night." And so, the first day began with evening and ended with morning.

Next, I made the heavenly layers stronger and gathered the waters below into one place, keeping the waves under control. From these waves, I formed large, solid stones, and from the stones, I shaped dry land, which I named earth. At the center of this land, I created a deep, endless pit.

I brought the sea together in one place and set a boundary for it, saying, "This is where you will stay forever. You will not cross the limits I have set for you." Then, I made the sky firm and placed it above the waters. This was the end of the first day.

When evening and morning passed, the second day began.

For the heavenly beings, I gave them a nature like fire. I looked at a strong, unbreakable stone, and from the brightness of My eye, I gave lightning its powerful glow. I placed fire within the water and water within the fire, making sure that neither would destroy the other. That is why lightning shines brighter than the sun, and soft water can wear down the hardest stone.

From the stone, I brought forth powerful fire, and from this fire, I created countless spiritual beings—ten thousand angels, each armed with weapons of flame and robes of burning light. I commanded them to take their places and follow the purpose I had set for them.

Translated by Tim Zengerink

Chapters XXIX. 4 - XXX. 3

[Here Satanail was hurled from the Heights with his Angels.]

One of the archangels, leading those beneath him, had a thought that could never come true—he wanted to raise his throne above the clouds and have the same power as Me. Because of this, I cast him down from the heights, along with his followers. Now, he wanders endlessly in the air above the abyss.

With that, I finished creating all the heavens, completing the third day. On this day, I commanded the earth to grow tall, fruit-bearing trees, towering mountains, and every kind of plant and seed. I also created Paradise, surrounding it with a protective barrier and placing fiery, armed angels at its entrance to guard it and keep it forever renewed.

When evening passed and morning arrived, it was the fourth day. On this day, I decorated the sky with great lights. In the highest circle, I placed the star Kruno. In the second, I set Aphrodite; in the third, Ares; in the fourth, the Sun; in the fifth, Zeus; in the sixth, Hermes; and in the seventh, the Moon.

I filled the sky below with countless smaller stars, making the Sun shine during the day and the Moon and stars glow at night. I gave the Sun its path through the signs of the Zodiac and set the Moon to follow the same twelve signs. I fixed their names, their purpose, and the timing of their movements—even the sounds of thunder and the precise passing of time.

When evening passed and morning arrived, the fifth day began. On this day, I commanded the sea to be filled with all kinds of fish and winged creatures. I also brought forth crawling creatures, four-legged animals, and everything that moves through the air. Each one was made male and female, given breath and life.

Finally, evening passed and morning arrived, marking the sixth day. On this day, I turned to My Wisdom and directed it to create man, forming him from seven elements.

Chapter XXX. 48

I shaped his body from the earth.
I made his blood from the morning dew.
His eyes came from the light of the sun.
His bones were formed with the strength of stones.
His thoughts were drawn from the speed of angels
    and the drifting clouds.
His veins and hair grew from the grass of the land.
And his spirit came from My own breath and the
    wind itself.
I gave him seven unique abilities:

His body could hear,
his eyes could see,
his mind could recognize scents,
his veins could feel touch,
his blood could taste,
his bones could endure,
and his thoughts carried both sweetness and wisdom.

I designed man with a perfect balance of what is seen and unseen. His life and death, his shape and spirit, all connected to both realms. Though his creation was small compared to My endless power, it carried a great and deep purpose.

I placed him on the earth as a being like no other, almost like an angel in human form. I gave him honor, strength, and glory.

I made him ruler over the earth, guiding it with My wisdom. Among all that I created, nothing else was like him.

Chapter XXX. 915

I gave him a name inspired by the four directions—East, West, North, and South.

I placed four guiding stars for him and named him Adam.

I gave him free will and showed him two paths—the path of light and the path of darkness. I told him, "This is good, and this is bad," so that his choices would reveal his heart. Through him, his descendants would also show their true nature, whether they loved Me or turned away.

Even though I understood his nature, he did not yet understand himself. This lack of knowledge became his struggle, leading him to make mistakes. Because of his wrongdoing, I declared that death would be the price to pay.

I put him into a deep sleep, and while he slept, I took one of his ribs and created a companion—his wife.

Through her, death entered the world, and I accepted what would become of his descendants. I gave her a name, calling her the mother of all living—Eve.

Chapter XXX. 16, 17

[Goel gives Paradise to Adam, and gives him Knowledge, so as to see the Heavens open, and that he should see the Angels singing a Song if Triumph.]

Adam lived his life on earth, and I created a garden in Eden, in the East, for him. I gave him the responsibility to follow My instructions and care for what I had given him.

I opened the heavens so he could see the angels singing songs of victory. In Paradise, there was always light—no darkness existed there.

But the devil, filled with jealousy, wanted a world of his own because everything on earth was under Adam's rule.

The devil, an evil spirit from the lowest places, became known as Satan after leaving heaven. Before his fall, his name was Satanail.

Though his nature changed, making him different from the angels, he still knew the difference between right and wrong. He fully understood the judgment against him and the sin he had committed.

Out of spite, he plotted against Adam and tricked Eve. But he never directly controlled or touched Adam.

Because of his evil plans, I cursed him for his arrogance and wickedness. However, I did not curse those I had already blessed.

I did not curse man, the earth, or anything I had created. Instead, I cursed the results of man's disobedience and the corruption that came from it.

Chapters XXX. 18 - XXXIII.1

[On account of the Sin of Adam, God sends him to the Earth, 'From which I took thee,' but He does not wish to destroy him in the Life to come.]

I told him, "You were made from the earth, and one day, you will return to it. I will not destroy you, but you will go back to where you came from. Then, when I return, I will take you again."

I blessed everything I created, both seen and unseen.

I also blessed the seventh day, the Sabbath, because on that day, I rested from all My work.

Chapter XXXIII. 26

[God shows Enoch the Duration of this World, 7000 Years, and the eighth Thousand is the End. (There will be) no Tears, no months, no Weeks, no. Days.]

Then I established the eighth day, making it the first after all My work was done. Let this day represent a time without end—no more counting years, months, weeks, days, or hours, but an everlasting age beyond measure.

Now, Enoch, everything I have told you, all that you have seen in heaven and on earth, and everything you have written—know that I created it all with My wisdom. From the highest places to the lowest, from the beginning to the end, I designed everything. No one advises Me or shares in My work, for I am eternal and not made by anyone. My thoughts never change, My wisdom guides Me, and My word is always true. I see all things, and when I look upon them, they remain as they are. But if I turn away, all things depend on Me to exist.

Listen carefully, Enoch, and understand who is speaking to you. Take the books you have written, for I will send you back with Samuil and Raguil, who brought you here. Return to the earth and tell your sons everything I have revealed to you—all that you have seen, from the lowest heaven to My throne.

I created all the heavenly beings and powers, and none stand against Me or disobey My will. Everything follows My command and exists under My authority. Give your writings to your sons, and they will read them and understand that I am the Creator of all things. They will know there is no other God besides Me.

Your writings will be passed down through their children, spreading across generations and nations. I will send you, Enoch, with My messenger, the great leader Michael, to keep these writings safe alongside the records of your ancestors—Adam, Seth, Enos, Kainan, Mahalaleel, and your father Jared.

These writings will not be needed until the final age.

For this reason, I have assigned two angels, Arinkh and Parinkh, to guard them on earth. They will make sure that the story of what happens to your family is not lost when the great flood comes.

Chapters XXXIII. 7 - XXXV. 1

[God accu.1es the Idolators; the Workers of Iniquity, such as Sodom, and on this account, He brings the Deluge upon them.]

I know how corrupt people will become. They will refuse to follow the path I set for them or use the gifts I have given. Instead, they will reject My guidance, follow another way, and invest in things that have no value. They will worship false gods and turn away from Me, the one true God.

The earth will be filled with evil, wickedness, and impurity. People will harm one another in terrible ways, committing sins too awful to name. Because of this, I will bring a great flood to wipe out everything, for the world will have become completely corrupt.

But I will save one righteous man from your family line, along with his household, because they will follow My ways. Over time, their descendants will grow into a large nation, though many among them will be consumed by their own selfish desires.

When their time ends, I will reveal to them the books you have written, along with the writings of your ancestors. The keepers of these books on earth will share them with those who are faithful to Me—those who respect My name and do not dishonor it. These people will pass the knowledge to the next generation, and those who read it will bring Me even greater glory.

Now, Enoch, I am giving you thirty more days to stay on earth and teach your family. Gather your sons and relatives before Me so they may hear your words. Let them read and understand that there is no other God but Me. Teach them to obey My commandments always and study the books you have written.

After thirty days, I will send My angels to take you away from the earth and from your sons, just as I have planned.

Chapters XXXV.2 - XXXIX. 1

[Here God summons an Angel.]

The angel standing beside me was a sight both breathtaking and terrifying. His appearance was as pure as freshly fallen snow, and his hands felt as cold as ice. The chill from his presence sank deep into my face, overwhelming me, for I could not bear the immense power of the Lord. It was like trying to withstand the heat of a blazing fire or the biting cold of the harshest winter.

Then the Lord said to me, "Enoch, if your face does not grow cold in this place, no human on earth could ever look at it and survive."

Meanwhile, my son Mathusal waited with hope, keeping watch by my bedside day and night, longing for my return. The Lord spoke to the ones who had taken me and commanded, "Return Enoch to the earth and remain with him until the appointed time." That night, they brought me back to my bed, where Mathusal had been keeping faithful watch. When he heard me return, he was filled with fear. I called for my whole household to gather because I had much to tell them.

With sorrow in my heart and tears in my eyes, I spoke to my children, filled with deep sadness.

"Listen carefully, my children, to the words given to me by the Lord. Today, I have been sent to you by Him to tell you what has happened, what is happening now, and what will take place before the day of judgment.

"Pay close attention, for these words are not my own. They come directly from the Lord, who has commanded me to share them with you. I am only a man, like you, but I have seen the face of the Lord. It was like metal glowing red-hot in a fire, sending out sparks that burned everything in their path."

"Look into my eyes, the eyes of a man who has been sent to deliver this message. I have looked into the eyes of the Lord, eyes that shine like the sun and fill the hearts of men with fear. Look at my hands, made of flesh like yours. I have seen the right hand of the Lord, a hand so powerful it stretches across the heavens, bringing help and support."

"My actions are human, just like yours, but I have seen the boundless, perfect form of the Lord, a form without limit or measure. You hear my voice, but I have heard the voice of the Lord. His words thunder like a storm, rolling through the sky with the power of roaring clouds."

"My children, listen to the words of your father. You know how terrifying it is to stand before a ruler on earth, knowing that your life or death depends on their judgment. But how much more fearsome, how much more overwhelming, is it to stand before the face of the Lord of all lords, the Master of heaven and earth? Who among us could ever endure such endless fear and trembling?"

Chapters XXXIX. 2 - XL. 6

[Enoch instructs fitfully his Children about all 1'hings from the Mouth of the Lo1'(l; how he Mw, and heard and wrote them clown.]

And now, my children, I want you to understand that the Lord has revealed everything to me. My eyes have seen all things, from the very beginning to the end of time. I have written down everything I have witnessed in my books—the vast heavens, their endless space, and the countless beings that fill them. I have studied the paths of the stars and recorded their movements, even though their number is too great to count.

No human has ever seen the full course of the stars, and not even the angels know how many exist. Yet, I have written down each of their names. I have measured the path of the sun and the strength of its rays, tracking its rising and setting throughout every month of the year. I have carefully recorded all its movements and given them their proper names.

I have also studied the moon's orbit, tracking its daily phases and the hidden places it retreats to before rising again. I have followed its journey through time, measuring its path by the hours. I have defined the four seasons and divided them into four great cycles. Within these cycles, I arranged the years, set the months in order, and from the months, counted the days. From the days, I measured the hours.

Beyond the heavens, I have observed everything that moves upon the earth. I have recorded every living creature, every plant that is sown or grows naturally, and all vegetation found in gardens. Every herb, flower, and fragrance has been written down along with its name.

I have studied how clouds form and move, how they gather water and release rain. I have observed how raindrops fall and documented everything I have learned. I have tracked the paths of thunder and lightning, and I was shown the forces that control them. I saw the guardians who hold the keys to these powerful forces, releasing them in measured amounts so they do not destroy the earth.

I have recorded the storehouses of snow and hail and studied the gentle breezes. I saw the keeper of these elements, how he fills the clouds with snow and hail without ever running out. I observed the places where the winds rest and watched their keepers carefully measure and release them, ensuring they do not shake the earth with too much force.

I have measured the entire earth—its tallest mountains, rolling hills, vast fields, and thick forests. I have recorded the stones, rivers, and everything that exists on the land. I measured the height from the earth to the seventh heaven and the depths down to the lowest place of judgment. There, I saw the great abyss open, filled with cries of despair, where souls suffer as they await their final judgment.

I wrote down the names of those being judged, recording the punishments they received and the actions that led to their sentence. Every deed and its judgment have been documented in my writings, preserving the truth of what I have seen.

CHAPTER XL. 713

[How Enoch wept for the Sins of Adam.]

I saw all the people who came before us, starting with Adam and Eve, and I felt a deep sadness. Tears filled my eyes as I thought about the harm their mistakes had caused. Overwhelmed with sorrow, I cried out, "How unlucky I am, struggling with my own weaknesses and the failures of those before me!"

In my heart, I thought, "The luckiest people are the ones who were never born—or if they were, never did anything wrong against the Lord. They would never have to see this place or suffer its pain."

Translated by Tim Zengerink

Chapters XLI. 1 - XLII. 6

[How Enoch Baw tho8e who keep the Keys, and the Guardians of the Gates of Hades standing by]

I saw the gatekeepers of hell, standing tall like giant serpents. Their faces were dark and empty, like lamps that had gone out. Their fiery eyes burned fiercely, their sharp teeth shone, and they wore nothing on their upper bodies.

I stood before them and said, "I wish I had never seen you or heard of what you do. I wish no one from my family had ever come to this place. The people of my kind have made mistakes during their short time on earth, but now they must suffer forever."

From there, I traveled east to the paradise of Eden, a place of rest prepared for the good and righteous. It is connected to the third heaven but is hidden from this world. At its grand gates, where the sun rises, stand powerful angels surrounded by flames. They sing songs of victory, celebrating endlessly in the presence of the just.

On the final day, Adam and our ancestors will be brought into this paradise. They will enter with joy, like guests invited to a great feast. Together, they will arrive with happiness, share in cheerful conversations, and eagerly wait for the celebration—a feast filled with never-ending light, endless blessings, and a life of joy and laughter.

Then I said, "Listen to me, my children: Happy is the one who respects the Lord's name and serves Him with honesty. Blessed is the one who gives offerings with a sincere heart, who lives fairly, and who dies in righteousness.

Blessed is the one who judges fairly, not for rewards but because they love what is right. In the end, they will receive true justice. Blessed is the one who gives clothes to those in need and feeds the hungry. Blessed is the one who treats orphans and widows fairly and stands up for those who have been wronged.

Blessed is the one who turns away from the temporary and unstable things of this world and chooses the path of goodness, leading to eternal life. Blessed is the one who does good deeds, for they will receive even greater rewards.

Blessed is the one who speaks truthfully and has a kind and loving heart. Blessed is the one who understands the works of the Lord and gives Him praise. The Lord's ways are always right, and while people may do good or bad, each person is known by their actions."

Translated by Tim Zengerink

Chapters XLII. 7 - XLIII. 2

[Enoch shows his Children how he measured and wrote out the Judgements of God.]

Listen, my children, to the wisdom I have gathered in my life and the lessons I have reflected on from the Lord. I have written these thoughts down through the seasons, both in winter and summer. I have studied the passage of time, measured the years and hours, and carefully recorded their changes.

Just as one year can stand out more than another, people also differ from one another. Some are respected for their wealth, while others are honored for their wisdom. Some are known for their deep understanding, while others are admired for their clever thinking. A person might be valued for speaking softly, another for having a pure heart. Strength makes some stand out, while beauty makes others shine. Youth brings energy, while sharp thinking brings recognition. Some are praised for their sharp senses, while others are admired for their ability to understand and learn many things.

But let everyone remember this: no one is greater than the one who respects and follows God. That person will be the most honored and will remain strong and righteous forever.

Chapters XLIII. 3 - XLF. 4

[Enoch instructs his Sons that they should not revile the Person, of men, whether they are great or small.]

God created people with His own hands, shaping them in His own image. He made both the powerful and the weak, and anyone who mocks another person's appearance is insulting God Himself.

If someone becomes angry at another without a good reason, they will face the Lord's great anger. If a person spits on someone in disrespect, they will stand before God's judgment and face its consequences.

Blessed are those who hold no hatred in their hearts. Blessed are those who defend the mistreated, support the accused, lift up the oppressed, and answer the cries of those in need.

For on the day of judgment, every act of fairness—every scale, measurement, and tool of justice—will be tested and will receive its true reward.

Translated by Tim Zengerink

Chapters XLVI. 1 - XLVIII. 1

[God shows that He does not wish Sacrifices from Man, nor Burnt Offerings, but pure and contrite Heart]

Whoever brings their offerings quickly before the Lord will also receive His blessings just as swiftly. God will ensure that justice is done for them. Whoever lights a lamp in His honor will find that their treasures in heaven grow even greater. But God does not actually need bread, light, animals, or any material gifts. These things have no real value to Him. What He truly desires is a heart that is honest and devoted. Through these offerings, He looks at what is inside a person's heart and tests their sincerity.

Think about how a king on earth would react if someone gave him a gift while secretly hiding bad intentions. If the king realized the person was being dishonest, wouldn't he reject the gift in anger and punish them? In the same way, if someone speaks kindly to another but secretly plans to hurt them, their deception will eventually be exposed, leading to shame. If people react this way, imagine how much more God despises and rejects gifts that come from dishonest hearts. He does not accept such offerings but instead turns away from them in anger.

One day, God will send a great light that will reveal everything. Both the good and the bad will be judged. No secret will remain hidden; every thought and intention will be exposed by His truth.

Now, my children, I urge you to keep these lessons close to your hearts. Think carefully about the words I have shared with you, for they do not come from me alone but from the Lord Himself. Hold on to these sacred teachings and study them carefully. In them, you will discover the incredible works of God. While many books have been written throughout history and more will continue to be written, none will reveal God's truth as clearly as these words.

If you follow these teachings and live by them, you will not turn away from God. Remember, there is no other God—nowhere in heaven, on earth, beneath the ground, or in the hidden depths of creation. Only He laid the unseen foundations of the world, stretched out the skies both visible and invisible, and set the earth upon the waters. He holds the waters in place without any solid ground beneath them, shaping everything in its endless beauty and variety.

Who but God can count every speck of dust on the earth, every grain of sand on the shore, every raindrop that falls, or each drop of morning dew? Who can measure the wind or control the land and sea with unbreakable laws? Who shaped the stars from fire, decorated the sky, and placed the sun at its center, giving it light and warmth for all? Only the Lord, the Creator of everything, has done these things and more. His power has no limits, and His wisdom is beyond understanding.

Chapters XLVIII. 2 - XLIX.1

[Of the course of the Sun throughout the seven Circles.]

The sun moves through the seven layers of the sky, and I have given it 182 positions for the days when its path is shorter and 182 for when its path is longer. In addition, there are two special positions where it rests as it moves between its monthly cycles. Starting in the month of Tsivan, after seventeen days, the sun begins to move downward until the month of Thevan. Then, on the seventeenth day of Thevan, it begins to rise again.

This is how the sun follows its path in the sky. When it comes closer to the earth, the land is filled with joy, bringing an abundance of life and fruit. But when it moves farther away, the earth becomes dull, and trees and plants stop growing. Everything follows a precise and perfect order, set by God's endless wisdom, both in the visible world and beyond what we can see.

From the unseen, He created everything we see,

though He Himself remains invisible. That is why, my children, I encourage you to share these writings with your families, your children, and people everywhere. Let those who are wise and respect God treasure these words. Let them value them more than the finest food, reading them with care and devotion.

But those who lack understanding and refuse to think about God will reject these teachings and turn away from them. For such people, judgment will come, and they will face the consequences.

Blessed is the one who accepts these teachings, carries them with faith, and follows them in life. That person will be free on the day of judgment and will stand in the light of truth and righteousness.

Chapters XLIX. 2 - LI. 2

[Enoch instructs his Sons not to swear either by the Heaven or the Earth; and shows the Promise of God to a Man even in the Womb of his Mother]

I tell you this, my children, with complete honesty. I will not swear by heaven, earth, or anything that God has made, because God Himself has said, "There is no swearing in Me, no injustice—only truth." If people do not have truth in their hearts, they should simply say "yes" when they mean yes and "no" when they mean no.

But I want you to know for certain—there has never been a single person born for whom a place has not already been prepared. Every soul has a purpose, and the time each person spends on this earth has already been set. So do not be misled, my children. Every soul has its own path and destination.

No one who has ever lived can hide from God, and nothing they do is truly secret. He sees everything, and I have written down the actions of every person. Each of us is given only a short time on earth, where we must face challenges and hardships. But during that time, we must never harm those who are vulnerable, like widows and orphans.

So, my children, live your days with patience and humility, and you will receive the gift of eternal life. Endure pain, hardships, and cruel words for the sake of the Lord. If someone wrongs you, do not seek revenge—not against a neighbor or even an enemy. Leave justice to God, for He alone will judge and repay when the time comes. Seeking revenge is not your place.

If any of you share your wealth to help a brother in need, you will be greatly rewarded on the day of judgment. Be generous to orphans, widows, and strangers, for acts of kindness are seen as treasures in the eyes of the Lord.

Chapters LI. 3 - LIII. 1

[Enoch instructs his Sons, not to hide their Treasures upon Earth, but lids them give Alms to the Needy.]

Help those in need as much as you can. Do not hide your wealth away—use it to support those who are honest but struggling. If you do, trouble will not come upon you when you face hardship. No matter what difficulties or challenges you must go through, endure them for the Lord's sake, and you will receive your reward on the day of judgment.

It is good to go to the house of the Lord in the morning, afternoon, and evening to honor the Creator of everything. Let all living things praise Him, and let every creature, seen and unseen, join in worship.

Blessed is the one who speaks to glorify the Lord and praises Him sincerely from the heart. But cursed is the one who uses their words to insult or harm others. Blessed is the one who lifts up God's name, but cursed is the one who spends their life speaking with anger, swearing, and showing disrespect.

Blessed is the one who appreciates and honors God's works, while cursed is the one who speaks badly about His creation. Blessed is the one who works hard and takes responsibility for their own efforts, but cursed is the one who relies on others without contributing. Blessed is the one who respects and upholds the traditions of their ancestors, while cursed is the one who disregards or destroys them.

Blessed is the one who brings peace and love among people. Cursed is the one who causes conflict and division. Blessed is the person who carries peace in their heart, not just talking about it but truly living it. However, cursed is the one who pretends to seek peace but secretly holds anger and resentment.

All these actions—both good and bad—are recorded, and on the day of judgment, everything will be revealed.

Chapters LIII. 2 - LVI. 1

[Let us not say that our Father is with God, and will plead for us at the Day of Judgment. For I know that a Father cannot help his Son, nor a Son a Father.]

Now, my children, do not think you can say, "Our father prays before God to free us from sin," because no one can take responsibility for another person's mistakes. Everyone is responsible for their own actions. I have recorded everything a person will do, even before they are born, just as it has been done for all people throughout time.

No one can change or erase what I have written, because God sees everything, even the hidden thoughts of those who do wrong. Nothing is truly secret from Him.

So, my children, listen carefully to my words. Do not ignore my advice only to regret it later and say, "Our father never warned us when we were lost in our foolishness." Pay attention now so that you do not look back with sadness, wishing you had known and done better.

Chapters LVI. 2 - LVIII. 5

[Enoch admonishes his Son that they should give the Books to Others.]

Let these books I am giving you be a gift of peace. Do not keep them hidden—share them with anyone who wants to learn. Encourage others to understand the incredible works of the Lord, which are beyond human understanding.

My children, my time with you is almost over. The moment is near when I must leave this world and go to heaven. Look, the angels are already here, waiting for God's command to take me. Tomorrow morning, I will go to the highest heavens, where I will live forever. So I urge you to do what is right in the eyes of the Lord and follow His ways.

Hearing this, Methuselah said to his father, "If it pleases you, Father, let me bring you food. Then, bless our homes, your sons, and our entire family so that your blessing may bring honor to your people. After that, you may go as God has commanded."

Enoch replied, "Listen, my son. Since the Lord anointed me with His glory, I no longer need earthly food. My soul has moved beyond the pleasures of this world, and I no longer desire anything from it."

Then Enoch said, "Call your brothers, their families, and the elders of the people so I may speak to them before I go, as the Lord has instructed me." Methuselah quickly gathered his brothers—Regim, Riman, Ukhan, Khermion, and Gaida—along with the elders of the people. They all came before Enoch, who blessed them and began to speak.

"My sons, listen to me. When the Lord first came to the earth for Adam's sake, He visited all of His creation. He gathered every animal, every creeping thing, and every bird in the sky and brought them before our father Adam. Adam named every living thing on earth, and the Lord made him ruler over all, placing everything under his care and commanding them to obey him. This is how God created man as the master of His creation.

But the Lord will not judge an animal because of a man's actions. Instead, He will judge people for how they have treated the animals. Just as there is a special place for every human soul, there is also a place for the souls of all creatures. Not a single soul that God has made will be lost before the great day of judgment. On that day, every animal will bear witness against the people who treated them unfairly, for the Lord sees everything and will judge with perfect justice."

Chapters LVIII. 6 - LIX. 4

[Enoch teaches all his Sons why they must not touch the Flesh of Cattle, because of what comes from it.]

Whoever treats animals cruelly or unfairly is also harming their own soul. When a person offers a clean animal as a sacrifice, they do so to protect their soul, recognizing that the life they take is meant for both nourishment and spiritual purpose. When done properly, this act is considered righteous and brings protection.

But if someone kills an animal carelessly or without respect, they hurt their own soul and commit a sin against themselves. It is a serious wrongdoing to harm any living creature without reason, as it reflects a heart filled with selfishness and cruelty. If a person secretly hurts an animal, it is an evil act that stains their soul, showing a lack of kindness and honesty.

Translated by Tim Zengerink

Just as it is wrong to harm animals, it is even worse to harm another human—whether by physical harm or through wicked intentions. If someone causes suffering to another person's soul, they also bring suffering upon themselves, leaving no hope for forgiveness. Taking another person's life not only destroys them but also ruins the soul and body of the one who committed the act, cutting them off from redemption forever.

Anyone who sets a trap for another person will eventually fall into it themselves because deceit does not go unnoticed by God. A person who attacks their neighbor—whether with weapons or with harmful words—will have to face judgment and will not escape punishment. Speaking unfairly or acting unjustly toward someone else is a serious offense that takes away any claim to righteousness.

My children, guard your hearts against all forms of wrongdoing, for these are the things the Lord rejects. Just as you ask God for mercy, you should also show kindness and compassion to every living being. Let your actions reflect the goodness you hope to receive. Help those in need, especially the poor, and give generously from the work of your hands. In the world to come, nothing will be hidden—God sees everything, both good and bad. So live with fairness, kindness, and truth.

Chapters LIX. 5 - LXII. 1

There are many places prepared for people after this life, each one suited to their actions—good for those who lived righteously and bad for those who lived in evil. These places are endless in number, representing the eternal future of every person. Blessed are those who are worthy to enter the homes of the righteous, where they will live in peace and everlasting joy. But those who are sent to the homes of the wicked will find no rest, no relief, and no hope of escape.

Listen carefully, my children, both young and old. When a person thinks good thoughts and offers gifts to the Lord from their own hard work, their offering must come from what they have earned through honest effort. If someone presents a gift that they did not work for, the Lord will reject it, and it will bring them no benefit. Likewise, if someone works but complains in their heart and gives unwillingly, their gift will not be accepted, and they will gain nothing from it.

When offering gifts to the Lord, do so with faith and sincerity. Blessed is the person who brings their offering with patience, humility, and devotion, for this act can help atone for their sins. But do not waste time with empty talk or delay doing what must be done, for missing the right moment leads to loss. After death, there is no chance to make up for missed opportunities—what is lost on earth is lost forever. Doing things at the wrong time offends both people and God because it shows disrespect for His divine order.

When you see someone in need, do not look down on them. Instead, help them with kindness and a sincere heart. When a person gives clothing to the poor or feeds the hungry, they earn a reward from the Lord. But if they give while complaining or with a reluctant heart, they commit two wrongs—they take away the value of their gift and lose their own reward. Those who receive help must also be careful, for if a poor person takes what is given with pride or ungratefulness, they waste the lesson of their hardship and miss the chance to be blessed in return.

The Lord despises arrogance and lies. Every proud or hateful word, every dishonest act covered in deceit, is offensive to Him. Such wickedness is like a sharp sword that cuts through truth, and it will be thrown into the fire to burn forever. So, my children, live with humility, honesty, and faith, so that your actions will be pleasing to the Lord and bring you everlasting reward.

Chapters LXII. 2 - LXV.2

[How the Lord call8 Enoch: the People take Counsel to go to kiss him in the Place called Achuzan.]

When Enoch spoke these words to his sons and the elders, news of how the Lord had called him spread quickly. People from near and far heard about it and said to one another, "Let us go and see Enoch and honor him!"

Around two thousand people gathered at a place called Achuzan, where Enoch and his sons were staying. The elders and leaders of the people approached Enoch with great respect. They bowed before him, kissed him, and said, "Enoch, our father, may the Lord, the eternal King, bless you! Today, we ask that you bless your sons and all of us here so that we may be honored in your presence."

They continued, "You, Enoch, are forever glorified before the Lord. God has chosen you above all people on earth and made you the scribe of His creation, recording everything that is seen and unseen. You stand against the sins of men and protect your family."

Enoch listened to them and then spoke these words to his sons and to all who had gathered:

"Listen carefully, my children. Before anything

existed, before any creature was made, the Lord created everything, both seen and unseen. When the right time came, He made man in His own image and likeness. He gave him eyes to see, ears to hear, a heart to understand, and the ability to think, make choices, and seek wisdom.

The Lord designed the world with mankind in mind. He created everything for man's sake, setting specific times for all things. From these times, He made years, from years He formed months, from months He shaped days, and from days He set seven in a cycle. Within these seven, He divided the hours into smaller parts so that man could understand the seasons and keep track of time—years, months, and hours. By knowing this, people could reflect on their lives from beginning to end, recognize their sins, and remember both their good and bad deeds.

For nothing is hidden from the Lord's sight. Each person must be aware of their actions and avoid breaking His commandments. Keep my writings safe and pass them down to future generations, for they contain wisdom and guidance for all.

When the time comes for all things, both visible and invisible, to reach their end—when the creation that the Lord Himself has made is completed—then all humanity will stand before Him in the great judgment. On that day, time itself will come to an end, and…"

Chapters LXV.2 - LXVI.1

There will come a time when days, months, years, and hours will no longer exist. Time itself will stop being measured. Instead, there will be one eternal age where all those who have lived righteously and escaped God's great judgment will be gathered together to live forever. These good and faithful souls will exist in endless joy and unity, with no end to their happiness.

In this eternal life, there will be no hard work, no sickness, no sadness, no fear, no hunger, and no darkness. There will never be another night. A strong and unbreakable wall will surround them, keeping them safe. They will live in a bright and perfect paradise, where everything that can decay or be destroyed will be gone forever. This paradise will be their home forever, filled with the light of the Lord, free from pain and suffering.

As Enoch spoke to his sons and the elders, he reminded them to live with deep respect for God and to avoid anything that goes against His ways. He warned them to protect their souls from all forms of wrongdoing, for the Lord despises evil. "Serve only the Lord," he said. "Do not worship idols or anything made by human hands. Worship the Creator, who made the heavens, the earth, and everything in them. God is everywhere—in the skies, on the earth, and even in the deepest parts of the sea. Nothing is hidden from Him. He sees all that we do."

Enoch encouraged them to live with patience, humility, and love. He urged them to endure suffering, insults, and temptations, knowing that these struggles were temporary and that their reward would last forever. "Blessed are those who escape the great judgment," he said. "They will shine seven times brighter than the sun, for they have been set apart as righteous."

He reminded them of the order of creation—how God separated light from darkness, created paradise, and prepared the fires of judgment. He recorded all these things so they could read and understand them. His writings were meant to guide them, helping them stay faithful to God's commandments.

After Enoch finished speaking, a great darkness covered the land, like a heavy cloud surrounding the people. Suddenly, angels appeared and carried Enoch up to the highest heaven, where the Lord welcomed him into His presence. As Enoch rose, the darkness disappeared, and light returned to the earth. The people who witnessed this amazing event did not fully understand what had happened, but they praised God and went home, telling others what they had seen.

Enoch was born on the sixth day of the month of Tsivan, and he lived for 365 years. On the exact day and hour of his birth, he was taken up to heaven, completing his life on earth. Before leaving, Enoch spent thirty days writing about all of God's creations, producing 366 books. He left these writings with his sons as a lasting gift of divine wisdom.

After Enoch was taken to heaven, Methuselah and his brothers built an altar at Achuzan, the place where Enoch had ascended. They made sacrifices to the Lord and invited all the elders and people to join in a great celebration. The people brought gifts to Enoch's sons, and for three days, they rejoiced, praising God for the incredible sign He had shown through Enoch, a man who had received an extraordinary blessing from the Lord.

This celebration and the story of Enoch's life were passed down through generations as a reminder of God's greatness and mercy. It served as a lesson for all to remain faithful to the Lord, to love and serve Him, and to pass His commandments from one generation to the next. Amen.

Thank You for Reading

Dear Reader,

We hope this timeless classic has sparked your imagination and enriched your literary journey. Now that you've turned the final page, we want to share a vision for the future of reading—one where every classic you've ever wanted to explore is at your fingertips, in a format that best suits your life.

We'd like to invite you to gain immediate, unlimited digital & audiobook access to hundreds of the most treasured literary classics ever written—along with the option to secure deluxe paperback, hardcover & box set editions at printing cost. Together, we can spark a new global literary renaissance alongside our small, independent publishing house called "The Library of Alexandria."

Thousands of years ago, the Library of Alexandria stood as a beacon of knowledge—until it was lost to history. We aim to reignite that spirit of preservation and discovery right now, in the modern age—only this time, it's accessible to all, in every language and every format.

Picture a world where every timeless classic, novel, poem, or philosophical treatise is not only available to read but also updated for today's readers—modernized, translated into any language or dialect, and ready to enjoy in any format you choose, whether that is in an eBook, audiobook, paperback, or deluxe hardcover & box set version a printing cost.

By joining our movement to rebuild the modern Library of Alexandria, you become part of an unprecedented mission to offer:

- **Unlimited Audiobook & eBook Access to the Greatest Classics of All Time**

    Instantly explore thousands of legendary works, from Plato and Shakespeare to Jane Austen and Leo Tolstoy. All are instantly ready to read or listen to, giving you a complete literary universe at your fingertips.

- **Paperback & Deluxe Editions at Printing Costs:**

    Purchase any title in a paperback, deluxe hardbound, or deluxe boxset edition at printing costs, shipped right to your doorstep. Curate your personal library of Alexandria with editions worthy of display—crafted to last, designed to captivate, and delivered straight to your door.

- **Modern translations for Contemporary Readers in all languages and dialects**

    Discover a vast selection of classics reimagined in clear, current language—no more struggling with outdated phrases or obscure references. Next to the original versions, we aim to offer translations in as many languages and dialects as possible.

    As we continue our translation efforts and add new languages, readers everywhere can connect with these works as if they were written today. By bridging linguistic divides, you're contributing to ensuring that these timeless stories become more meaningful, accessible, and inspiring for people across the globe.

- **Your Personal Library of Alexandria:**

    Over the months and years, you'll curate a unique physical archive of classics—each volume a testament to your taste, curiosity, and love of knowledge. It's not just about owning books—it's about curating a cultural legacy you'll cherish and pass down for generations to come.

- **Join a Global Literary Renaissance:**

    Your support fuels an ongoing mission: allowing us to reinvest in offering deluxe print editions (including special boxsets) at their true cost, broaden the range of available formats and translations, and extend the reach of these works to new audiences worldwide. By joining today, you're not just preserving a legacy of masterpieces; you set in motion a powerful wave of literary accessibility.

We are more than a publisher—we're a movement, and we can't do it alone. Your support lets us scale our mission, preserving and reimagining history's greatest works for tomorrow's readers.

Become a Torchbearer of knowledge.

Thank you for picking up this book and allowing us into your literary journey. As you turn the pages, know that you're part of something larger: a global effort to keep these stories alive, share their wisdom across borders and generations, and spark a true cultural revival for the modern era.

If this resonates with you—please consider taking the next step by visiting:

www.libraryofalexandria.com

With gratitude and a shared love of knowledge,

The Modern Library of Alexandria Team

Visit:

www.libraryofalexandria.com

Or scan the code below:

www.ingramcontent.com/pod-product-compliance
Lightning Source LLC
LaVergne TN
LVHW030631080426
835512LV00021B/3450